Fisl

Nottinghamshire

Published by:
Arc Publishing and Print
166 Knowle Lane
Sheffield S11 9SJ

Produced By: Chris Keeling

1

ISBN: 978-1-906722-19-7

ACKNOWLEDGEMENTS

I would like to thank the following for their
help in producing this guide:

Will Turner (Front Cover Photo)
Long Eaton Victoria Angling Society
Nottingham Anglers Association
Newark & District Piscatorial Federation
Worksop & District Angling Association
All fishery owners who have kindly
provided information.

August 2011

Arc Publishing and Print
166 Knowle Lane
Sheffield
S11 9SJ

W E L C O M E

Whether you prefer fishing still water lakes or the flow of a good river, Nottinghamshire has it all. The River Trent which dissects the county is one of the best coarse fishing rivers in the country. There are many stretches to choose from, many of which are run by angling clubs. The cost of joining these clubs is very reasonable, many of them have several waters including still water venues as well as rivers. The Nottinghamshire area has more fishing sites to choose from than most parts of the country. This can make it difficult to decide which one suits your way of fishing. Hopefully this guide will help you choose the right water for you.

Like many other anglers, my time on the bank is limited, but I like to grab a few hours fishing whenever and wherever I can. Always bearing this in mind, I have put together, my seventh book "Fish-it 7 Nottinghamshire".
I have included all the details you need to find the venues and hopefully give you an idea of what's on offer at each, before setting of on a lengthy (and now with petrol prices so high) expensive journey.

Fishing attracts so many people; perhaps it is the solitude in often beautiful surroundings, or the eager anticipation of catching a big one! The bank side can be almost hypnotic and the desire to catch just one more fish has spoilt many a meal.

I hope you find this book useful and wish you good luck, good fishing and remember -
"A bad day's fishing is still better than a good day's work!"

Chris Keeling

C O N T E N T S

ACKNOWLEDGEMENTS 2

WELCOME / CONTENTS 3

ABOUT THIS GUIDE 4

SPECIES / SYMBOLS..................................5

KNOTS 6

POLE FISHING FOR THE BEGINNER..........7

FISHERY LOCATION MAP 8

FISHERIES 9

RIVERS 49

FISHING TACKLE SHOPS 55

LOG-IT 56

FISHING TERMS 59

INDEX 62

NEW FISHERY / UPDATE FORM................63

A B O U T   T H I S   G U I D E

To help you locate a fishery, the venues have been arranged
in alphabetical order and split into two sections.
Their approximate location has been indicated on a map on
page 8

Blue Section   Nottinghamshire fisheries

Green Section   Nottinghamshire Rivers

Each page contains details of a fishery,
with information on the following:

Ticket Price: All day ticket costs plus details on OAPs,
                       disabled and junior concessions.

Directions: Usually from the nearest city or town, or
                       from the closest motorway junction.

Description: A brief outline of what the fishery looks
                       like plus details on features such as
                       islands, depths and the best
                       places to fish.

Types of Fish: List of species present, many with
                       estimated weights.

Rules/Bans: The restrictions set by the fishery
                       on type of baits, hooks etc.

Number of Lakes: The number of waters available to
                       fish at the venue.

Facilities: What is available at each location
                       i.e. cafe.

Telephone: The number of either the owner, angling
                       club secretary or match organiser.

Sat Nav: Post codes for use on satellite
                       navigation systems.

S P E C I E S / S Y M B O L S

Most commonly found in the Nottinghamshire area.

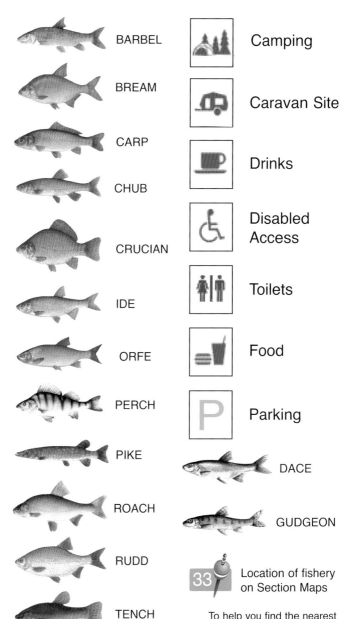

BARBEL

BREAM

CARP

CHUB

CRUCIAN

IDE

ORFE

PERCH

PIKE

ROACH

RUDD

TENCH

TROUT

Camping

Caravan Site

Drinks

Disabled Access

Toilets

Food

Parking

DACE

GUDGEON

33 Location of fishery on Section Maps

To help you find the nearest place to get tackle and bait, you will find a list of fishing tackle shops in the Nottinghamshire area on page 55

Blood Knot

This knot can be used to join two lines together, start by overlapping the ends of the two lines.

Thread the end of your line through the eye of your hook.

Twist one end round the other line four times and pass it between the two lines.

Pass the free end underneath the line and bring it back over the line to form a loop.

Do the same with the other end of line, making sure the previous step does not come undone.

Before pulling tight wet the knot to lubricate this also make it hold better. Trim off the two ends.

Half Blood Knot

Used mainly for joining hook to line.

Continue to loop the free end over the line about four times.

Pass the loose end between the eye of the hook and the first loop.

Pull on the loose end to tighten. Trim the line.

Double Overhand loop

This knot is used to create a loop at the end of a line. Also known as the surgeon's loop.

To begin, double the end of the line back against itself.

Tie an overhand knot in the doubled line.

The doubled end should then be tucked through the loop again.

Pull the knot as tight as possible and trim of the end.

Water Knot

This knot can also be known as the surgeon's knot. It is useful for joining a lighter hook line to your mainline

Hold the ends of the two lines alongside each other so that they overlap by about six inches.

Take hold of the two lines and make a wide loop.

Holding the two lines together. Pass the ends of the line through the loop four times.

Pull the lines tightly so that the loop makes a knot. Trim the two ends.

POLE FISHING
FOR THE BEGINNER

Of all the different methods of fishing I've tried, I haven't found any of them as accurate or as easy as pole fishing. To be able to place your bait and feed to the exact spot, sometimes only inches from an island or group of reeds is what makes pole fishing so productive and fun.

TACKLE NEEDED

A Pole

Poles come in various sizes, from 4 metres (usually called a whip) to poles of 18.5 metres. They also vary dramatically in price as well, this is usually governed by weight and rigidity. The lighter and straighter (no droop at the end) the more expensive they are. I recommend a pole between 11 and 13 metres, stay away from the smaller telescopic ones. Many tackle shops have poles ready assembled for you to handle, make sure you are comfortable with its weight and it feels well balanced. Test that it takes apart smoothly. If possible, get a pole with a spare top section as they enable you to rig up for different species and size of fish.

Pole Rigs

Experienced anglers can make up their own pole rigs but beginners are advised to buy ready-made. There are plenty of quality ready made rigs available for as little as £2.99. These rigs come with a main line with a loop on the end (used to attach the line to the stonfo connector at the tip of your pole). A float with enough shot below it to cock it nicely in the water and a length of lower breaking strain line, which has a spade end hook tied to it. The float and shot can slide down the line and be adjusted accordingly.

Pole Elastic

The elastic that runs through the top sections of your pole cushions the fight of a hooked fish and allows you to play it. Elastics are graded in sizes 1-20.
The following list is a good guide for the beginner:
1. For small roach and perch for example - use a No4 elastic with a 1lb hook length and a 2lb main line.
2. If fishing for small carp and tench or skimmer bream use a No8 or 10 elastic with a 3.5lb main line and 2.5lb hook length.
3. When fishing for carp up to 12lbs use a No16 to 18 elastic, and a main line of 8lb with a 6.5lb hook length.

START TO FISH

Fishing Position

Get your seatbox in position. Ideally, when sitting on the box, your thighs should be in a horizontal position, at right angles to your lower leg. Holding the pole correctly makes it comfortable for long periods and prevents backache. For a right handed person you need to rest the pole across your knees with your left hand supporting it. Put your right forearm along the end of the pole and firmly grip the pole with your right hand. Have close to hand - your bait, landing net, disgorger and anything else you may require for your days fishing. It is important to have your pole roller in the correct location. The pole has to be well balanced in your hands when it leaves the roller - this prevents rig tangles when shipping out.

Start Fishing

You have set up your pole and plumbed your depth - so now you are ready to fish. Make sure you have between 10" and 20" of line between the tip and float. In more windy conditions you may want to lengthen this. Feed your swim with groundbait (if allowed) plus a few bits of your hook bait. This is more accurately done using a pole cup which can be fixed to the end of your pole. Put your bait on the hook and ship out your pole trying to keep your rig in the water as this prevents tangles. Lay the rig on the water lengthways. The shot on the line will pull the line under the water and cock the float.
Enjoy your first pole fishing day!

Fishery Location Map

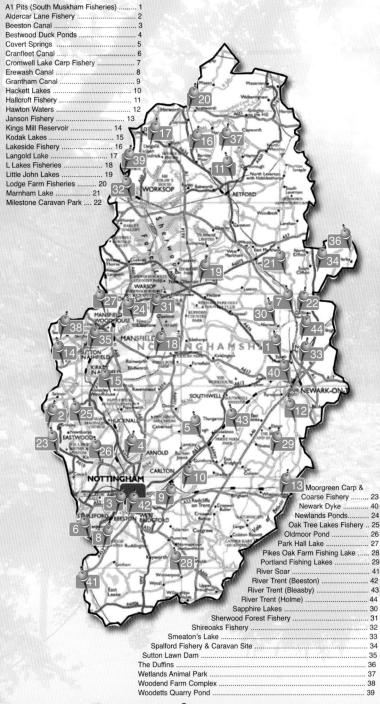

A1 Pits (South Muskham Fisheries) 1
Aldercar Lane Fishery 2
Beeston Canal 3
Bestwood Duck Ponds 4
Covert Springs 5
Cranfleet Canal 6
Cromwell Lake Carp Fishery 7
Erewash Canal 8
Grantham Canal 9
Hackett Lakes 10
Hallcroft Fishery 11
Hawton Waters 12
Janson Fishery 13
Kings Mill Reservoir 14
Kodak Lakes 15
Lakeside Fishery 16
Langold Lake 17
L Lakes Fisheries 18
Little John Lakes 19
Lodge Farm Fisheries 20
Marnham Lake 21
Milestone Caravan Park 22

Moorgreen Carp &
   Coarse Fishery 23
Newark Dyke 40
Newlands Ponds........... 24
Oak Tree Lakes Fishery .. 25
Oldmoor Pond 26
Park Hall Lake 27
Pikes Oak Farm Fishing Lake 28
Portland Fishing Lakes 29
River Soar 41
River Trent (Beeston) 42
River Trent (Bleasby) 43
River Trent (Holme) 44
Sapphire Lakes 30
Sherwood Forest Fishery 31
Shireoaks Fishery 32
Smeaton's Lake 33
Spalford Fishery & Caravan Site 34
Sutton Lawn Dam 35
The Duffins 36
Wetlands Animal Park 37
Woodend Farm Complex 38
Woodetts Quarry Pond 39

A1 Pits (South Muskham Fisheries)
Church Lane, South Muskham.

SAT NAV NG23 6EQ

Ticket Price: £5 for 12 hours. £10 for 24 hours
An additional charge of £5.00 per 24 hours applies to caravans. This covers you for up to 4 rods.
All money is collected by the Bailiff on the bankside, there is no pre-booking required.

Directions: Exit A1 at the B6325 / Newark. At the roundabout take the third exit onto the B6325. Turn left onto Church Lane. Go through the village, then straight after the railway lines turn right into the fishery. Access to the river is by the same route just keep going past Pit 6 and turn right.

Description: With six pits and a stretch of the River Trent to fish there's a lot to choose from. Pit 1 is the smallest and an ideal starting ground for beginners, coarse fishermen or introducing your children to the sport. The pits go up in size from 1-6. All are deep, going down to 25 feet in some places. This venue is heaven for the serious carp angler with some monsters at around 39lbs coming out of Pit 5. As well as large carp, A1 has plenty of big pike the biggest to date at 37lb.

Rules/Bans:
See details on site.

Number of Lakes: Six + a stretch of river. **Sat Nav:** NG23 6EQ

Facilities: [P] [caravan] **Telephone:** (Bailiff) Tel: 07970209433

Aldercar Lane Fishery
Aldercar Lane, Aldercar.

Ticket Price: Adults £6.00 Concessions £4.00
Get your day tickets before fishing - available from the club house.

Directions: From Eastwood take the A610 signposted Ripley. After 1.5 miles turn left onto Cromford Road.
Take your second left onto Aldercar Lane. Follow the lane for another 1.5 miles and look for the fishery on your right.

Description: There are 4 lakes in total; The Folly, The Railway, The Acorn and The Snipe.
The lakes are well stocked with a variety of fish including carp, chub, bream, roach, tench and rudd. This relatively new fishery is maturing nicely. The reeds near most pegs are ideal to fish up to. Even the large carp can be caught at your feet. If that fails try fishing corn at 10 metres from the bank. This is becoming a popular match venue, so check there are spare pegs for pleasure fishing at the weekends.

Types of Fish: Carp, chub, bream, roach, tench and rudd.

Number of Lakes: Four

Rules/Bans: Only pellets purchased on site are to be used. Barbless hooks - maximum size 10. No floating baits, boilies, meat of any kind, blood worm or joker to be used. Landing nets to be used at all times.
No keepnets allowed - except in matches. Dip all nets before and after use.
No night fishing. No braided line. No pole method.

Facilities:

Telephone: 07779 253502　**Sat Nav:** NG16 4HJ

Beeston Canal
Willow Road, Nottingham.

Ticket Price: Day tickets £3.00. Concession £1.50. Nottingham AA run this section of canal. Full Member £40.00. Disabled or over 65 £30.00. Juniors (age 15 or under) £10.00. Permits are available from local tackle shops.

Directions: From the A52 Dunkirk roundabout continue along the A6005 Abbey Street towards Nottingham. At the traffic lights turn right into Lenton Lane and continue for 500 yards, then turn right into Willow Road. After 200 yards park where the River Leen goes under the road. Walk down the footpath alongside the river for 150 yards to the canal. The association water is to the left (upstream) of where the river goes under the canal.

Description: Over 150 pegs of very good canal fishing to the west of Nottingham City Centre. Being joined at both ends to the River Trent means that all the species found in the river can probably be found in the canal. Roach and bream are the predominant species, however, large chub often show up along with the odd carp. There are many points of access and good towpaths make certain lengths ideal for anglers with disabilities.

Types of Fish:

Rules/Bans: Night fishing is not allowed. No closed season. Open all year.

Number of Lakes: One

Facilities:

Telephone: 0115 9199500

Sat Nav: NG7 2TA (to nearest industrial unit)

Bestwood Duck Ponds
Moor Road, Bestwood Village, Nottingham.

SAT NAV NG6 8UJ

Ticket Price: This is a Nottingham AA water and membership is required to fish the pond. Full Member £40.00. Disabled or over 65 £30.00. Juniors (age 15 or under) £10.00. Permits are available from local tackle shops.

Directions: From Nottingham follow Hucknall Road to Moorbridge, then just before the bridge turn right at the traffic lights into Bestwood Road. Continue along this road through Bestwood Village, approx ½ mile beyond the village look for Goosedale Lane on the right. The entrance to the ponds is 50 metres beyond this.

Description: A fantastic set of five ponds, which consist of:
Pond 1. This is a general coarse lake and is noted for the large water lilly beds that are home to tench in excess of 8lbs. Also resident are carp, bream, roach, rudd, perch, chub, barbel and pike. There is an average depth of 4-5ft.
Pond 2. Although this could be classed as the general coarse lake, this is the one to fish for the large carp and pike.
Ponds 3&4. These lakes contain a general mix of coarse fish and are surrounded by very comfortable pegs. Depths vary from 5-12ft and access around the ponds is quite easy.
Pond 5. Another mixed coarse lake with some specimen carp present. This lake has far more weed growth in the summer months than the other lakes creating another challenge for those that fish it.

Rules/Bans: See individual rules for each pond.

Number of Lakes: Five

Facilities:

Telephone: 0115 9199500 **Sat Nav:** NG6 8UJ

Covert Springs
Epperstone by pass, Epperstone.

Ticket Price: Specimen lake day tickets £10.00, or £5.00 for 5 hours. Coarse lakes £7.50 or 7am to 12.00pm £3.50.

Directions:

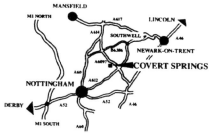

Description: This very attractive three lake fishery caters for both the young novice angler and the more experienced carp fisherman. The small Specimen Lake can only be fished by four anglers at a time. It has carp up to 32lbs and plenty of large tench. Try using mussels for the carp; no poles allowed on this lake. The other two lakes both hold carp and various silver fish. A lovely spot where children are welcome. There's even a pony and an alpaca roaming the grounds. This well kept, clean fishery is well worth a try.

Rules/Bans:

Number of Lakes: Three

Facilities:

PLEASE NOTE
NO Barbed or Bent Hooks (Strictly Prohibited)
NO Keep Nets
NO Ground Bait/Boiles/Hemp
NO Tiger Nuts/Peanuts/Seed Baits
NO Dog or Cat Meat
NO Trout Pellets
NO Method Feeding
Use of Two Rods at One Time Only
ALL Fish MUST be Returned to the Waters
PLEASE Leave Pegs Tidy/Litter Free

Sat Nav:
NG14 6DH

Telephone: 0115 9663839

Cranfleet Canal
Long Eaton.

Ticket Price: Day ticket price £2.50

Directions: From Long Eaton town centre, follow the Tamworth Road towards Sawley (and the station). Pass under the railway bridge at the station, remain on the Tamworth Road for ½ mile, then turn left (signposted 'Trent Lock'). Follow road to car park at end (over rail crossing, past golf club on right, boat yard on left). Park by the Navigation Inn. On foot, pass to left of 'Navi' and follow path to bridge over Erewash Canal's 'Trent Lock'. Cross bridge, turn right, follow path to end of canal, bear left at River Trent, and after 30yds you reach the entrance to Cranfleet Canal.

Description: All methods can produce fish, but I recommend pole, light waggler or light bomb, size 16 or smaller hooks, maggot, worm or bread punch over loose feed. The pegs nearer to the river have produced excellent bags of large bream, as well as large carp, chub and barbel during the warmer months and pike during the winter.
Main species are roach, bream and perch, but there are pike, carp, chub, tench and eels present.

Rules:
No fishing allowed between the bridge and the downstream lock gates which are used for permanent moorings.
Fishing is restricted to the upper end of the canal, from the bridge crossing it up to the River Trent. There are no permanent pegs. Take care to avoid overhead power lines. As Cranfleet is linked to the River Trent, no fishing is permitted from 15 March to 15 June inclusively.

Telephone: 0115 972 8547 Long Eaton Victoria Angling Society.

Cromwell Lake Carp Fishery
Cromwell, Newark.

Ticket Price: Specimen Lake. Day Ticket £12.50. 24 Hour £25
Match Lake. Day Ticket £6.00. 24 Hour £12

Directions: Head north from Newark on the A1. Take the exit at Cromwell, drive towards the village and take your first left. Follow the road over the A1 and you will see the fishery.

Description: Cromwell has a fantastic 18 acre spring fed specimen lake set in beautiful surroundings containing good head of fish including 40lb+ mirror carp, 35lb+ common carp, 30lb+ ghost carp, 20lb+ grass carp, 30lb+ pike, 25lb+ wells catfish and 10lb+ channel catfish. There's also lots of double figure tench with a lake record of 14lb 6oz.
The fishery also has a small pleasure pond containing a large head of fish including roach, rudd, ide, crucians, stillwater barbel, perch, golden orfe, tench and carp.

Rules/Bans: Barbless or micro barbed hooks. No carp in keepnets. All nets must be dipped. No dogs. No littering. More rules are on site for the Specimen Lake.

Number of Lakes: Two   **Sat Nav:** NG23 6JE

Facilities: P ☕ ♿ 🚻   Shop, cafe and caravan site nearby.

Telephone: Mob: 07535 631324 Tel: 01636 822425   7

Erewash Canal

Long Eaton. Long Eaton Lock down to Trent Lock.

Ticket Price: Day ticket price £2.50

Directions: The Canal runs adjacent to the Tamworth Road, Long Eaton, and may be accessed at any point between the Fire Station and Canal Bridge. Park where permitted, along the Tamworth Road or any of the side roads leading off it, or behind the 'Old Ale House' pub (after seeking permission).

Description: There are large fish throughout this stretch, most of the biggest specimens are taken from the Trent Lock end, with the exception of the big perch which show throughout the whole length. Pole tactics are most popular, although rod and line (with waggler) can also produce, as can ledgering for the big carp. Successful baits are; maggots, squats or pinkies, casters, hemp, tares, worms and bread. The fish will respond to both loose feed and groundbait in moderation. Leger hair rigged meat for the larger carp.

Types of Fish: This is an excellent canal fishery, and contains the following species: Roach (to 1 lb), perch (to 3 ½ lb), chub (to 6 lb), bream (to 5 lb), gudgeon, carp (to 20 lb), tench and pike (to 20 lb).

Rules/Bans:
Fishing is only permitted from permanently marked pegs. Live baiting on society canal fisheries is strictly prohibited.

Telephone: 0115 972 8547
Long Eaton Victoria Angling Society.

Grantham Canal
Lady Bay to Cotgrave, Gamston, Nottingham.

Ticket Price: Day tickets £3.00. Concession £1.50 for Lady Bay to Tollerton Lane and Cotgrave Road to Hollygate Lane. The section from Tollerton Lane to Cotgrave Road is Nottingham AA Members only. Full Member £40.00. Disabled or over 65 £30.00. Juniors (age 15 or under) £10.00. Permits are available from local tackle shops.

Directions: From Grantham take the A52 to Nottingham. When you reach the Gamston roundabout continue straight on to Nottingham on the A6011. Go over the canal bridge on Ratcliffe Road and park. Other parking at Cotgrave Road, Hollygate Lane and Tollerton Lane.

Description: Grantham Canal is an non-navigable canal that runs from Nottingham to Grantham. Because of the shallow water and the lack of boats a lot of the canal has reed and weed growth. There are however one or two very good sections where the weed growth is not too bad and these hold a lot of fish. Without doubt the most abundant species in the canal are tench; early mornings and late evenings providing some very good sport. Roach, bream, perch and pike are also present.

Rules/Bans: Night fishing is not allowed. No closed season, Open all year.

Number of Lakes: One

Telephone: 0115 9199500

Facilities: P

Sat Nav: NG12 3HB (Cotgrave end)

Hackett Lakes
Adbolton Lane, Holme PierrePont.

Ticket Price: £6.00 for 1 Rod, £7.00 for 2 Rods.

Directions: Leave Nottingham heading south on A60 London Road, turn left onto Cattle Market Road and then right onto County Road. After approximately 0.2 miles, turn right onto Meadow Lane and then right again onto Lady Bay Bridge. Continue along Radcliffe Road towards Holme Pierrepont. Turn left onto Regatta Way and then onto Adbolton Lane. Continue until you reach Hackett Lakes which are clearly signposted on the right hand side.

Description: Lake 1 is the smaller of our two fishing lakes and is an ideal match lake. As recently as 2005 it was stocked with carp reaching up to 20lbs in weight. Abundant perch, chub and roach are also found in the reeds while the tench tend to favour the deeper water.
Lake 2 was also stocked with similarly sized carp and offers the keen angler some of the best fishing in the area. It's a lovely unspoilt setting thats close to Nottingham.

Types of Fish: Roach, bream, rudd, carp to 26lbs, chub, tench, crucian and perch.

Number of Lakes: Two

Rules/Bans: All fishing is on a strict catch & release policy. Fishermen must use barbless hooks only, no fishing with live bait. Please take all your litter home with you. Dogs must be kept on a lead and away from the water.

Facilities: 🚻 ♿ P

Telephone: 07798 702 053
Sat Nav: DNG12 2LD

18

Hallcroft Fishery
Hallcroft Road, Retford.

Ticket Price: Day Tickets - Adult £6.00. OAP's £5.00. Junior - £4.50.

Directions: Head south from Bawtry/Doncaster on A638. As you approach Retford turn left into Randall Way. Continue to the end T Junction. Turn Left onto Hallcroft Road, continue to the end and turn right into the fishery.

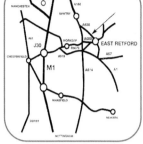

Description: Hallcroft offers everything the pleasure and match angler could need. A total of 6 lakes and a small stretch of the River Idle (400 pegs). There is a 100 seater cafeteria with licensed bar, that serves breakfasts.
Male, female and disabled toilet facilities, plus a shower block for those anglers staying overnight.
There is plenty of parking and for disabled anglers you can park your car behind nearly every peg on the venue.
If it's big carp you're after try these two ponds.
Moat Pool: 190 pegs. Stocks are 60% carp & 40% silver fish. Carp up to 20lbs, bream to 8lbs, perch to 3lbs.
Bridge Pool: 80 pegs. Stocks are 60% carp & 40% silver fish. Carp up to 27lbs, perch to 3lbs.

Barbel, chub, dace and gudgeon in the river.

Rules/Bans: Barbless hooks only. No method/Inline or fixed feeders. No floating baits. No braided lines. All nets must be dipped prior to fishing. Keepnets (matches only). See notice for further rules and baits bans.

Number of Lakes: Six   **Sat Nav:** DN22 7RA

Telephone: 01777 710448

Facilities:

Hawton Waters

Cotham Lane, Hawton, Newark.

Ticket Price: Lake fishing - £5.00 per day. Extra rod - £1.00 per day. River fishing £5.00 per day.
Syndicate membership £250.00 per year.

Directions: Head south out of Newark on Hawton Road. Continue along this road for about three miles. Go straight through Hawton village. The fishery/caravan site is a further mile along the road.

Description: Hawton Waters caravan and motorhome leisure breaks has lake side / lake view pitches. Fishing of the lake and river is permitted to private syndicate members and leisure break visitors. This is not a day ticket venue.
The lake is stocked with an array of fish including mirror, common, leather and ghost carp, with recent catches of 38lb (Big Betty!!) as well as bream, roach, rudd, tench, eel and pike. The river catches include chub, bream and carp.

Types of Fish:

Bans/Rules: Barbless hooks only. No keepnets.

Number of Lakes: One, plus a stretch of river.

Facilities: 12

Telephone: 01636 704742   **Sat Nav:** NG24 3RJ

Janson Fishery
Redmile Lane, Elton.

Ticket Price: Day tickets are £5.00. £4.00 concessions.

Directions: Coming from Nottingham, travel on the A52 towards Grantham. After Whatton look for the Vale of Belvoir pub on the right and turn off the A52 there. Go past the pub entrance on the left and round the corner - the next entrance on the left is the fishery.

Description: Tomo's pool is a well matured pond with 16 pegs. This irregular shaped pond has an island running down the middle. It has a large head of mixed species including carp to 28lb, tench, barbel, chub, roach, rudd and crucians. With depths ranging from 2 to 5 foot, pole or waggler tactics are the best to adopt on Tomo's Pool. Best baits include chopped worm, caster, pellet and sweetcorn. There are two other ponds to try. Pool One which is an ideal 'lads and dads' lake and Pool Two which is the match lake.

Types of Fish:

Rules/Bans: No keepnets, barbless hooks only. There are too many rules to list but please read the rules on site.

Number of Lakes: Three

Sat Nav: NG13 9EU

Facilities:

Telephone: 07976 317864 (general info)
07971 191103 (specific angling info)

Kings Mill Reservoir
Kings Mill Lane, Sutton in Ashfield.

SAT NAV NG17 5HZ

Ticket Price: Day tickets £3.00. Concession £1.50. Nottingham AA run this reservoir. Full Member £40.00. Disabled or over 65 £30.00. Juniors (age 15 or under) £10.00. Permits are available from local tackle shops. Closed season from the 15th March to the 31st April

Directions: Follow the A60 north towards Mansfield. At the large junction just before West Notts College turn left onto the A617. Go straight on at the next set of lights, travelling slightly down hill towards the A38. The entrance to the car park is on the right. For the dam end continue down to the A38 and turn right at the traffic lights. At the next set of lights turn right again heading towards Mansfield. Kings Mill Lane is on the right after about 1/3 mile.

Description: A very large but shallow reservoir containing some very big carp. Fish to 30lb have been reported but are elusive due to night fishing not being allowed on this water. Roach, bream and hybrids and some pike are also present, The pegs at the dam end where the depth is around 6ft give the best chance of success.

Types of Fish: Carp, roach, bream, pike

Rules/Bans: Night fishing is not allowed on the reservoir.

Number of Lakes: One

Telephone: 0115 9199500

Sat Nav: NG17 5HZ
(to nearest house at Kings Mill Lane end)

Facilities:

Kodak Lakes
Lakeview Drive, Annesley.

Ticket Price: This is a Nottingham AA water and membership is required to fish the pond. Full Member £40.00. Disabled or over 65 £30.00. Juniors (age 15 or under) £10.00. Permits are available from local tackle shops.

Directions: From Hucknall continue north along Annesley Road and onto the A611 towards Annesley. From the A611 roundabout continue for 2 miles to the traffic lights and turn left towards the M1 (J27). At the next roundabout turn right and then left into Lakeview Drive. The lakes are on the left after 500 Yards.

Description: These well maintained lakes, although in the middle of the Sherwood Enterprise Park are a very pleasant place to fish. The two drainage lakes adjacent to the now redeveloped former Kodak factory are relatively shallow and the banks are quite flat making them the ideal place to teach junior anglers. Good fishing for anglers of all abilities. For younger or more inexperienced anglers the large amounts of small fish almost guarantee bites when fishing with maggot. There are however many carp, bream, perch and the occasional tench and golden orfe that can often take anglers by surprise.

Rules/Bans: No keepnets. Barbless hooks only.

Number of Lakes: Two

Telephone: 0115 9199500

Sat Nav: NG15 0DT

Facilities:

Lakeside Fishery

Access Road, Ranskill, Nr Retford.

Ticket Price: Coarse lake £5.00. Pensioner £3.00
Carp lake £7.00 per day. £7.00 per night.
Trout Lake £9.00 catch+release. £13.00 for 2 fish, £18 for 4

Directions: From the A1 junction 34 head towards Blyth on
Bawtry Road. In Blyth turn left onto Retford Road. After half a
mile turn left onto Blyth Road. Continue onto Station Road,
cross the railway line and turn right for the fishery.

Description: There are five lakes at the Lakeside Fishery
complex, comprising a 40-peg match lake, two pleasure
lakes, a specimen lake and even a fly lake. The match lake
holds carp to double figures, ide, skimmers, tench, roach,
bream, rudd, chub and crucians, providing year-round sport.
Pole fished pellet, meat or caster tends to produce the best
weights on this lake. Anglers fishing pole with baits
presented shallow will do well when fishing the smaller strip
ponds, while anglers tackling the Specimen Lake using
fishmeal or fruit-flavoured boilies do best, taking carp to over
22lb.

 16

Rules/Bans:

COARSE LAKE
1. ALL LANDING NETS TO BE DIPPED IN TANK OUTSIDE. NO KEEPNETS ALLOWED.
2. BARBLESS HOOKS ONLY.
3. NO HEMP OR TARES
4. GROUNDBAIT IN FEEDER OR POLE CUP
5. ONLY ONE ROD TO BE USED AT ANY TIME.
6. NO FIXED OR BOLT RIGS
7. NO HOOK LENGTHS STRONGER THAN MAIN LINE.

BAILIFF WILL INSPECT AT REGULAR INTERVALS.
ANYONE BREAKING RULES WILL BE TOLD TO LEAVE IMMEDIATELY.

Number of Lakes: Five

Facilities:

Telephone: 01777 818524

Sat Nav: DN22 8LW

Langold Lake
Off Church Street, Langold.

Ticket Price: Day tickets £4.40.
Season Ticket 1 April to 31 March: £60

Directions: From Worksop take the A60 Tickhill Road north for 5 miles, passing through Carlton in Lindrick, Costhorpe and into Langold Village. Ignore the first turn off the main road, and continue to the first proper left turn (Ramsden Avenue). Turn immediately left again onto Church Street. Continue along here - the main car park is at the end.

Description: This old estate lake is run by Bassetlaw District Council. Langold is noted for its tench and bream, the latter of which run to double figures. Even if there is a match on the lake there is still plenty of room for pleasure anglers. Pike to double figures with plenty of jacks to live bait around the dam end. The concrete wall is very popular with the locals as this is the deepest area. There are lots of natural pegs with lillies, a distinct advantage when fishing for tench. The only downside can be the amount of walkers on a sunny day.

Types of Fish: Roach, tench, bream, pike to around 28lb - and some big perch.

Rules/Bans: Keepnets to be used only during matches. Barbless hooks only.

Number of Lakes: One

Sat Nav: S81 9NW
to nearest house

Facilities:

Telephone: 01909 730910

L Lakes Fisheries
Lind Close, Rainworth, Mansfield.

Ticket Price: Adult day tickets £5.00. Juniors £3.00. Blue badge holders £4.00. Available on the bank. Night fishing by prior arrangement £20.00. Season permits available.

Directions: Head towards Rainworth on the A6191 from Mansfield. At the large roundabout take the B6020 signposted Rainworth. Turn right into Lake Farm Road. Take your next right into Lind Close and bear left at the end. Follow the lane to the fishery.

Description: Main Lake and Match Lake are the names of two waters. Main Lake at around 6 acres has carp to 35lbs, bream to 9lbs, large tench to 10lbs as well as good sized perch, roach and chub. Match Lake is much smaller at 1.5 acres with 28 pegs This lake is packed with fish and is more suited to the novice angler. Meat, large pellet or boilies will catch the carp. Float fishing with corn works well for the tench. A nice attractive venue with disabled access, toilets and both food and bait available on site.

Types of Fish:

Rules/Bans: Barbless hooks only. Two rods only.

Number of Lakes: Two   **Telephone:** 07792 549381

Facilities: ♿ P 🥤 🚻   **Sat Nav:** NG21 0ED

Little John Lakes
Maida Lane, Ollerton.

SAT NG22 9RG NAV

Ticket Price: Adult £6.00. OAP's and disabled £5.00. Under 16's £4.00 if accompanied by an adult. Tickets from the cabin before fishing.

Directions: Take the A616 from Newark to Ollerton. At the roundabout take the second exit. Once you pass the police station turn left into Walesby Lane. Turn left again just over the speed calming hump onto Dove Croft. Follow the road to the large iron gates of the fishery.

Description: There are three lakes at this very popular fishery, Robin Hood, Maid Marion and the newly constructed Frier Tuck. All lakes are of a similar size and have around 27 pegs on each. I fished Robin Hood lake which has an average depth of 4 feet and was told had the larger fish in it. I struggled to reach the island in front of my peg using a pole, so fished the reed margins. After limited success and a few to many gudgeon, I switched to feeder fishing up to the middle of the three islands. After a few minutes I caught my first of many carp weighing around 4lbs. Check before travelling that there are pleasure pegs available as this is a busy match venue.

Rules/Bans: Landing nets supplied and must be used on all fish. Barbless hooks. No keepnets except in matches. No litter. No braid to be used. No night fishing.

Number of Lakes: Three   **Telephone:** 01623 835581   19

Facilities: ♿ 🅿 🥤 🚻   **Sat Nav:** NG22 9RG

Lodge Farm Fisheries

A638 Great North Rd, Scrooby Top, North Notts.

Ticket Price: Day Tickets £5.00.
Concessions £3.50. Match £6.00.

Directions: Lodge Farm is situated on the border of South Yorkshire and North Nottinghamshire. Come out of Bawtry heading south on the A638. Lodge Farm is on the left just before Ranskill.

Description: Five great ponds at this venue with the top pond having mixed coarse fish with 46 pegs and depths of around 15 feet. The Lily Pond and Long Pond has mainly carp, chub, and bream with around 30 pegs each.
Field Pond has 38 pegs with carp , bream, chub and barbel.
Signal Lake has also got carp, bream, chub and a good head of tench. An excellent cafe has recently opened on site and is worth a visit.

Types of Fish: Carp, chub, bream, tench, barbel and some recently introduced ide.

Rules/Bans: No keepnets (except matches),
All nets must be dipped on site, Barbless hooks max size 12, no in line or running method type feeders, no nuts, boilies, bloodworm or joker. All litter must be taken from the site.

Number of Lakes: Five

Facilities:

Telephone: 0781 5030694   **Sat Nav:** DN10 6AX

Marnham Lake

Holme Lane, Marnham.

Ticket Price: Day ticket prices for pleasure fishing are £5 for adults and £4 for under 16's and concessions.

Directions: From Dunham Bridge. Once over the bridge go through the village heading towards the A1. About 1 mile from the bridge, take the right hand turn at the crossroads signposted "Ragnall ½m". Once you've taken the turn, follow the road through Ragnall for about 2½ miles until you pass a right turn for "Polly Taylor's Road". Shortly after at the junction, take a left hand turn. Follow the road for about ½ mile and at the junction, take the right turn (signposted "Low Marnham" and "Marnham Lake").

Description: This oval shaped lake has 54 pegs and is ideal for the pole fisherman. Fishing to the island which is easily reached should see you bag up on carp with many of them reaching double figures. There's also a good head of ide, with most other silver fish species present.
Marnham have just opened the venue for campers and caravaners, so if you want a few nights away this could be the venue for you!

Rules/Bans: No keepnets except in matches.
All landing nets & keepnets must be dipped and rinsed! (vats are positioned on entry to the lake) No dog or cat food (biscuits or meat). Night fishing is not allowed!
No littering, please take all your rubbish away with you!

Number of Lakes: One   **Telephone:** 07747 020564

Facilities:

Sat Nav: Not available.

29

Milestone Caravan Park
Great North Road, Cromwell, Newark.

SAT NG23 6JE NAV

Ticket Price: £4.00 per day (dawn until dusk) per person

Directions: From Newark take the A1. After 5 miles you will see a petrol station, just before it you will see a slip road and a sign that says 'Cromwell' & 'Gravel Works'. Take the slip-road and follow the road all the way through the village. Roughly 150yds past the brewery you will see Milestone Caravan Park on your left.

Description: At Milestone they cater for all types of anglers; from the family fisherman to the more seasoned anglers.
The lake is well stocked with carp, tench, perch, roach, rudd and bream so there are most varieties to catch.
There are plenty of reed bed features to target on this caravan site pond. Try these margins with sweetcorn or luncheon meat for the plentiful carp.

Types of Fish: Carp, tench, perch, roach, rudd and bream

Rules/Bans: One rod per person. No keepnets.
No ground bait. Barbless hooks only. Please fish from the platforms only.

Number of Lakes: One

Facilities:

Telephone: 01636 821 244   **Sat Nav:** NG23 6JE

Moorgreen Carp & Coarse Fishery
Greasley Estate, Willey Lane, Eastwood.

SAT NAV NG16 3QW

Ticket Price: The carp fishery is run on a members only basis. A full day/night permit is £300 and £275 for renewals. The coarse fishery membership permit is £80. Day tickets for the coarse fishery are available at £7. Bought in advance from the fishery, no paying on the bank (contact the fishery). Permits run for 12 months from the date of purchase.

Directions: From Junction 27 M1, take the A608 exit to Heanor/Hucknall. At the roundabout take the exit onto A608/Mansfield Rd heading to Heanor. Continue onto the B600/Willey Lane. After about 1 Mile you will pass the reservoir dam wall on your left; take the next left.

Description: Two choices at this venue, either the 38 acre reservoir which runs down the valley or the 4 acre lower pond. The reservoir is mainly for the serious carp angler. There are some huge fish in here and plenty of them. One fish regularly comes out over 40lb. The coarse fishing pond is an old estate lake. Depths range from 2 feet to 12 feet with the average 7-8 feet at two rod lengths from the bank. Fish stocks are pike to 25lb+, tench to 6lb, roach, rudd and perch, there is also 15 to 20 carp to 25lb.

Bans/Rules: Check the numerous rules before purchasing a permit or day ticket.

Number of Lakes: Two   Sat Nav: NG16 3QW
                                   to nearest house

Facilities:

Telephone: 0776 968 3057 (water bailiff)

Newlands Ponds
Crown Farm Way, Clipstone.

Ticket Price: Membership of Nottingham AA is required to fish these lakes. Full Member £40.00. Disabled or over 65 £30.00. Juniors (age 15 or under) £10.00. Permits are available from local tackle shops.

Directions: Take the A614 north to Rufford. At the Rose Cottage Pub turn left and continue to a set of traffic lights and turn left. Continue along this road for a few miles through Kings Clipstone and New Clipstone. At the next roundabout turn left into Crown Farm Way. At the bottom of the dip turn left into a bridleway and the entrance to the ponds is on the right.

Description: A series of four lakes with excellent parking and access. Most anglers are attracted to the ponds by the prospect of the very good roach and skimmer fishing on offer. Large nets of skimmers to 2lb are quite common place when using pellet, paste or small pieces of luncheon meat. Carp well in excess of 10lbs are also present along with tench, perch and the odd chub.

Types of Fish: Carp, roach, bream, tench, perch, gudgeon and chub.

Rules/Bans: Ground baiting is allowed only in moderation. Night fishing is strictly prohibited and the use of bivvies or boilies is not allowed.

Number of Lakes: Four

Telephone: 0115 9199500

Sat Nav: NG19 0FT

Facilities:

Food outlet nearby.

32

Oak Tree Lakes Fishery

Cordy Lane, Brinsley.

SAT NAV NG16 5BZ

Ticket Price: Adults - £6 per day. Over 65's and blue badge holders - £5 per day. Under 16's - £3 per day (under 14's to be accompanied by an adult)

Directions: From Junction 27 of the M1. Take the A608 to Underwood. As you leave Underwood turn right onto Cordy Lane. The fishery is a few hundred yards on your left.

Description: Oak Tree Lakes is a friendly, family run business. Comprising of Ash Pond which has been established over 100 years and will accommodate 15 fishermen and Oak Lake, which houses 27 custom built platform pegs. The fishery caters for both match and pleasure fishing offering a scenic and relaxed setting. The well-stocked waters include a variety of carp, tench, bream, skimmers and perch among others.

Types of Fish: Carp, roach, tench, perch and bream.

Rules/Bans: Please pay before fishing. Dip all landing nets prior to fishing (located between ponds). Barbless hooks only. Do not handle fish with rags and keep contact to a minimum. No hemp, boillies or floating baits. No floating poles. Ground bait used only in feeders and pole pots No keepnets. Please dispose of all litter. Strictly no night fishing. Do not leave baited rods unattended in the water. Strictly one rod or pole per person. No dogs.

Number of Lakes: Two   **Telephone:** 01773 775860

Facilities: Sat Nav: NG16 5BZ

Oldmoor Pond
Strelley Village.

Ticket Price: This is a Nottingham AA water and membership is required to fish the pond. Full Member £40.00. Disabled or over 65 £30.00. Juniors (age 15 or under) £10.00. Permits are available from local tackle shops.

Directions: From the A6002 Woodhouse Way. Turn right at the traffic lights into Strelley Village, follow the road through the village past the church on the right. Approx 200 metres past the church there is a left turn onto a bridleway, follow this track over the motorway.
The entrance to the pond is on the left just over the bridge. Follow the track to the bottom of the hill. There is ample parking at the bottom of the track.

Description: A small pond with 30 pegs which is situated close to the M1 motorway. Large stocks of fish include roach, rudd, bream, perch and crucian carp. Common and mirror carp to 20lbs are also present and many fish fall to floating baits during the summer months. Depths range from 3ft on the motorway side to 7ft on the woodside.

Types of Fish: Carp, roach, rudd, bream, crucian carp, perch,

Rules/Bans: No keepnets. Barbless hooks only.

Facilities: P   **Number of Lakes:** One

Sat Nav: Not available   **Telephone:** 0115 9199500

Park Hall Lake
The Fairways, Mansfield Woodhouse.

SAT NAV NG19 9EW

Ticket Price: Adults £5.00. Extra rod £3.00 each.
Children under 16 £3.50 (accompanied by adults only)

Directions: Situated off the A60 Mansfield to Warsop road.
Turn off onto 'The Fairways', 50 yards from 'The Spikes' pub
and golf course. The entrance is quarter of a mile on your
right.

Description: This previously private well kept fishery is ideal
for the pole angler who want to target the many lily pads that
are in front of many of the pegs. Towards the far end of the
lake the water opens out giving the feeder or ledger angler
more space to catch the good sized carp that are present.
Very good pegs with parking available behind most. Got to
be worth a visit if only for the large quantity of good sized
tench.

Types of Fish:

Rules/Bans:

PARK HALL LAKE
FISHING RULES

BARBLESS HOOKS ONLY
NO BLOODWORM
NO CATMEAL
NO TROUT PELLETS
NO DOGS
NO FIRES
NO NIGHT FISHING
NO FISH TO BE REMOVED
NO SPINNING

Number of Lakes: One

Facilities:

Telephone:
01623 653082
07831 447434

Sat Nav: NG19 9EW

Pikes Oak Farm Fishing Lake

& Caravan Site, Willoughby Road, Widmerpool.

SAT NAV NG12 5PU

Ticket Price: Day tickets £7.00. Reduced rate of £5.00 per day for those staying on site. Senior citizen's £6.00

Directions: Leave the A46 at the junction with A606. Head towards Nottingham. After 200 yards turn left signposted Widmerpool. At T-junction turn left through village, turn left again signposted Willoughby. The site is 500yds on your left.

Description: Situated in a secluded and tranquil location on the Nottinghamshire/Leicestershire border, this caravan site pond is ideal for the novice angler. There are plenty of reed bed corners to target the carp and tench.

Pole fishing with sweetcorn or meat baits seemed to be working well for most anglers. A couple of guys were feeder fishing into the centre of the pond and I did see one of them pull out a carp to around 10lb.

Types of Fish: Bream, tench, carp, rudd and roach

Rules/Bans: No keepnets. Barbless hooks only.

Number of Lakes: One

Facilities:

Sat Nav: NG12 5PU

Telephone: 0115 9372283

Portland Fishing Lakes

Longhedge Lane, Sibthorpe, Near Newark.

Ticket Price: Day Tickets £5.00. (concession available for under 16's or 65 & over - please ask the bailiff)

Directions: From the village of Shelton, head towards Flintham. Before reaching the crossroads at the bottom of the hill, take a right turn just after the woods and turn up the unmade road - the entrance is post and rail fenced with a metal barrier. Continue up the road between the fishing lakes and the car park and clubhouse will then come into view.

Description: There are four lakes located just outside the village of Sibthorpe, with more planned. Portland has great facilities including a cafe offering a top class breakfast. A new bait bar is now on site. Toilet facilities for ladies, gents and people with disabilities. Luncheon meat works well on the Old Wood Lake, with plenty of catches around the 12lb mark. Carp to 30lb, barbel to 10lb.

Types of Fish: Barbel, tench, bream, chub, carp, perch, roach and rudd.

Rules/Bans: Keepnets only in matches. Barbless hooks only. Max hook size 12. No floating baits. No cat or dog meat. No boilies or nuts. Children under 14 must be supervised.

Facilities: Sat Nav: NG23 5PN

Number of Lakes: Four   **Telephone:** Bailiff 0781 8552307

37

Sapphire Lakes
Norwell Lane, Cromwell, Newark.

SAT NAV NG23 6JQ

Ticket Price: Carp lake £10.00. Prior booking only.
Stock pond and match lake £6.00 a day.

Directions: From Nottingham take the A52 towards
Grantham. At the main Bingham island join the A46 to
Newark. Join the A1 - North. Exit the A1 at Cromwell.
Take a left turn signposted Norwell. Turn left just before rail
crossings to Sapphire Lakes.

Description: The carp lake is a picturesque 4.5 acre lake with
many features, especially in the summer when the lilly pads
are at their peak. There are 18 pegs and it holds a good
head of double figure carp to 32lb. There is always a good
chance of getting that elusive 20lb plus fish on this lake. The
stock is roughly 50/50 commons and mirrors. All the carp
are the original stocked British fish.
All baits work well, especially the old favourite "fake corn".
The lake averages 6-7ft with some areas going to 9ft.
Margin fishing is not to be ignored, especially at night.
The match water at the fishery provides the angler with 28
pegs and holds a good stock of carp, tench, bream and
roach. Depths vary on this lake from 2 - 3 feet in the
margins to 14 - 15 feet towards the centre of the lake.

Rules/Bans: Children must be accompanied by an
adult. No dogs. Barbless hooks only. No cat or
dog meat. No nuts.

Sat Nav: NG23 6JQ

Facilities: **Night fishing available.**

Telephone: 01636 821131   **Number of Lakes:** Three

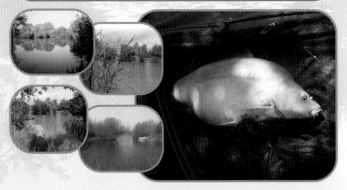

Sherwood Forest Fishery

Sherwood Forest Farm Park, Clipstone.

Ticket Price: Adult 1 rod £6.00. 2 rods £8.00.
Juniors (16 and under) £4.00. OAPs £5.00

Directions: Take the A60 out of Mansfield and join the A6075 signposted Edwinstowe. At the Warsop double roundabout turn right signposted Clipstone and Sherwood Forest Park. After 200 yards turn right into the Farm Park entrance signposted fishing and follow the signs down the lane.

Description: Out of the five waters to try at Sherwood my favourite is oblong shaped Cavendish Lake at around 1 acre in size and with 25 pegs. It's reed fringed and 60m wide from one bank to the other. The depth is 3-4 foot with the deepest end being at peg 1. A mixed lake with roach - 1lb, carp - 24lb, rudd, tench, big gudgeon and lots of skimmer bream - that leap out of the water when you strike. Pole, waggler and the feeder all work well throughout the year but the pole fishing down the margins or out to 11m is best. Sweetcorn, meat, maggots and paste all produce well over a bed off carp pellets.

Rules/Bans: No boilies, nuts, peas or beans. Carp pellets only. No braid. Barbless hooks, maximum size 6. All kinds of meat based pet food is banned at the fishery. No floating baits.

Facilities: ♿ P ☕ 🚻 Camp site near by. 31

Telephone: 0772 1316334   **Sat Nav:** NG21 9HL   **Lakes:** Five

Shireoaks Fishery

Shireoaks Common, Shireoaks, Nr Worksop.

Ticket Price: Day tickets £5 then £1 for every extra rod - max three. Pay on the bank.

Directions: Head out of Worksop on the A57 towards the M1. Turn left at the roundabout signposted Shireoaks. Follow the road called Shireoaks Common through the village, over the railway line. When you reach the church, the road goes to your left, at this point go straight over. After a few yards bear left into the fishery.

Description: Shireoaks has two ponds to try. The one you see on your left as you come through the gates is the match lake. It's around two acres with an island in the middle and packed with silver fish and good sized carp. Beware it can get busy at weekends. The specimen lake behind the pub which is on site has most species of carp, including grass carp at nearly 30lb. I recently fished this lake with a strong margin pole, while waiting for my bite alarm to go off on my carp rod and pulled out three of the smaller carp, each over 10lb.

Types of Fish: Various species of carp. Bream, roach, rudd, chub, and tench.

Rules/Bans: No keepnets, barbless hooks only. No night fishing. Other rules apply.

Number of Lakes: Two   **Sat Nav:** S81 8LT

Facilities:

32

Telephone: 01909 500979

Smeaton's Lakes

Great North Road, Newark.

Ticket Price: Carp lake £6.00 (2 rods)
Coarse lake £5.00 (2 rods) River £6.00
Extra Rod £1.00 (max 3)
Children (under 14 yrs) £3.00
Children to be accompanied by an adult.

Directions: Situated just outside
Newark-on-Trent on the A616 Great North Road.

Description: Smeaton's Lakes is the ideal place for your fishing and touring needs. Set in 90 acres and four waters to try. Finger Pond – 21 pegs, so called because of its shape is stocked with pike with coarse fish in abundance. Sawmill Carp Lake – 15 pegs is stocked with common, mirror and leather carp. The larger, stronger fish in this specialist carp lake will keep the most demanding fisherman busy for a while. Burrows Coarse Lake - 20 pegs and Reed Pond Coarse Lake – 40 pegs. These two coarse lakes contain many species such as bream, chub, small carp, perch, roach, rudd, tench and orfe.
River Trent - There are 7 pegs along the river, which is noted for barbel, bream, chub and carp.

Rules/Bans: No keepnets, except during matches.
No barbed hooks. See other rules on site.

Number of Lakes: Four, plus a stretch of the River Trent.

Facilities: ☕ 🚻 🅿 ♿ 🚐   Night fishing available.

Telephone: 01636 605088   **Sat Nav:** NG23 6ED   33

Spalford Fishery and Caravan Site
Eagle Road, Spalford, Nr Newark.

Ticket Price: Day tickets £5.00.
The price is reduced later in the day.

Directions: From Newark take the A1133 north. Turn off at the signpost for Spalford Village. Drive along Sand Lane into the village. As you leave the village the lane turns into Eagle Road, follow the road until you see the fishery on your left hand side.

Description: This small lake of about 3/4 of an acre, has recently been re-stocked with carp up to 4lbs and a huge quantity of F1's. Most other species are present in this water with good heads of roach, rudd and crucian carp. The island in the centre can be reached from most pegs and this is where the larger carp can be found. An ideal venue for a few days away camping or caravaning.

Types of Fish: Crucian carp, tench, roach, rudd, perch, bream and carp.

Rules/Bans: Barbless hooks only. Dawn until dusk fishing only. Keepnets can be used during cooler months.

Number of Lakes: One

Telephone: 07774 770127   **Sat Nav:** NG23 7HA

Facilities:

Sutton Lawn Dam
Sutton Lawn Pleasure Grounds, Sutton in Ashfield.

SAT NAV
NG17 4LS

Ticket Price: Senior Day Ticket - £4. Junior/Disabled / OAP Day Ticket - £2. Club Membership (Season Ticket) - £40. Concessions for OAP's, Disabled - £30. Under 16s - £20. Matches booked at £4 per peg.

Directions: Sutton Lawn Dam is the lake in Sutton Lawn Pleasure Grounds, the home of the Ashfield Show. From Junction 28 of the M1, head towards Sutton in Ashfield/Mansfield on the A38. Turn left at the 6th set of traffic lights onto Station Road (B6021) heading towards Sutton in Ashfield. Take the 2nd turning on the right opposite Aldi/Homebase, signposted Sutton Lawn Pleasure Grounds. Drive through the park over speed bumps until you see the lake on your right hand side. The carpark is situated on the right at the bottom of the hill, just before the care home.

Description: Ashfield Angling Association run the water very well. Most pegs seem to be alive with silver fish. Skimmers and roach nudge a pound, with tench to 5lb, and bream to 4lb. A good number of double figure commons and mirrors being reported. The water depths range from around 3 feet on the Lawn side to 10 feet on the Sheepwash side and then back to 3-4 feet at Mickey's side.
There is a wildlife section where fishing is not permitted.

Rules/Bans: No bloodworm or joker. No nut baits allowed. Barbless hooks only. No live baiting. No baited lines to be left unattended (in or out of the water). No fish over 3lb to be kept in keepnets (except in a match) No carp or pike allowed in keepnets. No fishing without a landing net.

Number of Lakes: One   **Facilities:**

Telephone: 07912 315308   **Sat Nav:** NG17 4LS

43

The Duffins
Main Street, Thorney.

Ticket Price: Day ticket £6.00

Directions: From Lincoln take the A57 heading north / west. After around six miles look out for the signpost for Thorney on your left. Follow Roadwood Lane for one mile. Once you have passed a few houses, look out for the ponds on your right hand side.

Description: Thorney, as a lot of people call these two very similar natural ponds are about one acre in size. Both have islands in the centre and are stocked with the same fish. The pond on your right does have the larger carp, which are easily caught using pellet or luncheon meat. Try fishing close up to the islands or next to the margin reeds. If you get your bait to the bottom before the hoards rudd grab it, you will have a chance of catching one of the many 5 - 10lb mirror and common carp. Plenty of reasonable sized tench are present as well as a good head of crucian carp.

Types of Fish: Carp, rudd, tench, roach, crucian carp.

Rules/Bans: Landing nets must be dipped. Barbless hooks only. No floating bread. No method feeders. No night fishing. No keepnets. No boilies. No groundbait. No litter.

Number of Lakes: Two   **Telephone:** 01522 702257

Facilities: P   **Sat Nav:** NG23 7DD
to nearby house.

44

Wetlands Animal Park

Lound Low Rd, Lound, Near Retford.

SAT DN22 8SB NAV

Ticket Price: Day Ticket £6.00.

Directions: From Retford take the A638 North Road. After nearly two miles turn right into Sutton Lane. Continue onto Town Street, through Sutton Village. After one mile turn right onto Lound Low Road. Stay on Lound Low Road until you see the Animal Park on your left.

Description: Two excellent lakes set within 32 acres of Wetlands Animal Park. Main Lake has 48 pegs and is used for fishing matches, although pleasure anglers are able to use the lake on a Tuesday and Thursday. Back Lake is available for pleasure fishing every day except bank holidays. There are 30 pegs and the lake has a mixed variety of fish with weights up to 30lb.

Types of Fish: There are roach, perch, bream, tench, carp and ide with match winning weights of up to 160lb.

Rules/Bans: Barbless hooks only. No method feeders. No blood worm. No joker. No floating baits. No cat meat. No dogs.

Number of Lakes: Two   **Sat Nav:** DN22 8SB

Facilities:

Telephone: 01777 818 099

Woodend Farm Complex
Off Chesterfield Road, Huthwaite, Sutton-in-Ashfield.

SAT NG17 2QJ NAV

Ticket Price: Day tickets are £6.00 (£2 for an extra rod)

Directions: Only 3 miles from Junction 28 of the M1 motorway. Take the A38 to Mansfield and then turn left to Huthwaite on the B6027. Follow the signs for Tibshelf. The ponds are situated near the 'Woodend Inn' pub.

Description: This coarse fishery is open all year round with no closed season. There are 5 lakes set in lush green surroundings. The ponds are all stocked with tench, roach, bream, rudd and all the carp family. The Donut Pond is a 30 peg pond stocked with all the above species with 10 - 15lb fish being caught regularly. The Kidney Pond holds a good supply of fantastic silver fish as well as carp to 17lb. The Bottom Pond is a secluded pond surrounded with trees. The carp are recorded to be 25lbs+ with plenty of 2lb and 3lb roach and bream being caught on a regular basis. Lastly there is the Match Pond which holds all the carp family and all the other species mentioned.

Types of Fish: Carp, bream, tench, roach and rudd.

Rules/Bans: No keepnets (unless in approved match) No sharing of landing nets. No hemp or floating bait. No night fishing. No liquidised bait, artificial bait or bread. No cat or dog food. Nets must be dipped. Hooks must be barbless.

Facilities:

Number of Lakes: Five   **Sat Nav:** NG17 2QJ

Telephone: Office: 01623 550544   Mobile: 0780 7503335

Woodsetts Quarry Pond

A57, Gateford Road, Worksop.

Ticket Price: Adult day tickets £3.00, 2 rods £5.00. Concessions £1.50.

Directions: The lake is easily found on the A57 just before the first major roundabout heading into Worksop from the M1. There is no sign, but look out for a metal gate on your left.

Description: This gravel pit, old quarry is around 5 acres. The water is favoured by the carp angler, who can place his bait in the centre, avoiding the heavy weed that surrounds the lake. Try fishing to the right of the carpark, where you will find a few lily pads to fish up to. This is a nice, quite attractive venue but the water is very clear.

Types of Fish: This mixed coarse fishery produces pike to 27lbs. Both carp and catfish are present.

Rules/Bans: See notice board at the side of the lake.

Number of Lakes: One

Sat Nav: Not available.

Facilities:

Telephone: 01909 486350 (Worksop & District AA)

A few more to try

Nottinghamshire has many more fisheries than I can possibly fit in this guide. Here are a few details on further waters you could try. If you have any up to date information on these or other venues, please fill in the form at the back of the book.

Attenborough Gravel Pits. Operated by Nottingham Anglers Association. Permits available from most local tackle shops. Species of fish at venue: Bream, Perch, Pike, Roach,Tench.
T: 0115 9199500

Bank End Fishery. Near Finningley, North Notts.
Three lakes, good mixed fishery. Well stocked match lake.
T: 01302 770224 Sat Nav: DN9 3NT

Barkers Pond, Long Eaton. Take B540 Tamworth Road towards the town centre. Turn right at Wyvern Avenue. Permits available: From the bailiffs on the bank.
Species of fish at venue: Bream, carp, pike, roach, tench
T: 05602 380254

Barnstone Lakes Fishery. Permits available from Matchman Supplies. Species of fish at venue: Carp, mixed coarse.
T: 0115 923 3412 or 07906 493397

Chesterfield Canal - Drakesholes Tunnel & West Retford Bridge. Operated by Worksop and District AA.
Species of fish at venue: Bream, chub, roach.
T: 01909 486350

Clumber Park - Clumber Lake. Worksop.
Permits available: Estate office
Species of fish at venue: Bream, carp, perch, roach, tench
T: 01909 476592

Colwick Park. Nottingham. Operated by Colwick Park Fishing Lodge. Permits available from the lodge.
Species of fish at venue: Bream, pike, roach.
T: 0115 9870785

Martins Pond & Raliegh Pond. Located in the Wollaton area of Nottingham. Carp to 36lbs, bream to 12lbs, roach to 2lbs, tench to 9lbs, rudd to 1lb, perch to 4lbs. Run by Wollaton Piscatorial Club. Adults £2.50. Oap's £2.00. Junior £1.50
T: 07530 926593

Winfield Lagoon - Holme Pierrepoint.
Species of fish at venue: Bream, carp, perch, tench.
T: 0115 982 1212

Sandhill Lake. Operated by Worksop and District AA
Species of fish at venue: Bream, eels, roach, rudd, tench.
T: 01909 486350

Willow Holt Farm - Newark. On A46 between Farndon and East Stoke. Species of fish at venue: Carp T: 01636 525265

Newark Dyke

River Trent, Newark on Trent.

Ticket Price: ● Day Ticket £4 payable on bank to bailiff.
(No Concessions) ● Members only waters.

Directions: For areas C & D, access is via Long Lane which is first right after the Lord Ted pub roundabout. Go straight over the mini roundabout until you reach the river.
For E,F & G, access is first right after the large roundabout near the Lord Ted pub. Turn right at the mini roundabout and follow the road into the car park at the end of the un-surfaced section. For area H, park on the path at the side of the hedge or in the approach to Dorner Avenue at the weekends. Walk across the field, or go up Dorner Avenue and access the field by the footpath between the houses.
For K & L, access is over Mill Bridge off Millgate, park on left and walk over the stone bridge. For area M, access is over the footbridge at the Aldi supermarket. For P & N park under the A1 bridge at Winthorpe by driving along the bank at Winthorpe Rack (where parking is allowed behind the pegs). For Q, access is immediately over the Winthorpe Railway Crossing over a cattle grid, drive over grid and park in the field behind your peg.

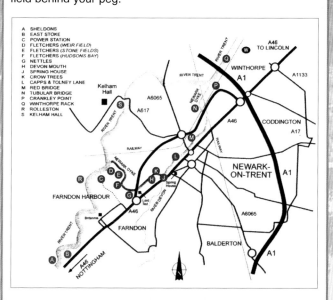

A SHELDONS
B EAST STOKE
C POWER STATION
D FLETCHERS (*WEIR FIELD*)
E FLETCHERS (*STONE FIELDS*)
F FLETCHERS (*HUDSONS BAY*)
G NETTLES
H DEVON MOUTH
J SPRING HOUSE
K CROW TREES
L CAPPS & TOLNEY LANE
M RED BRIDGE
N TUBULAR BRIDGE
P CRANKLEY POINT
Q WINTHORPE RACK
R ROLLESTON
S KELHAM HALL

Information kindly supplied by Newark & District Piscatorial Federation

49

Description: Most of the waters can be fished on a day ticket purchased on the bank from the various bailiffs. There are exceptions to this on a few stretches that are available to members only. The Kelham stretch can be fished by non members who have purchased tickets in advance.

The permanent pegs installed 30 yards apart, using flat Matlock stone in the form of steps to accommodate varying water levels are excellent.

The largest barbel known from the Fletchers Weir stretch weighed 15lbs. 2oz. Carp to 25lbs. plus have been caught and a large shoal of bream inhabits this water. Roach, chub (to 6lbs.) and perch predominate. Barbel are increasingly being caught all along the stretch.

Types of Fish:
Bream, roach, tench, carp, chub, perch, pike and barbel.

Telephone:
01636 702962

Sat Nav:
Not available

River Soar

Beeby's Meadow and Woodside, Near Kegworth.

Ticket Price: This is a Nottingham AA water and membership is required to fish the river. Full Member £40.00. Disabled or over 65 £30.00. Juniors (age 15 or under) £10.00. Permits are available from local tackle shops.

Directions: From Clifton Bridge continue along the A453 for six miles. Just after the Ratcliffe Power Station turn left into Kegworth Road and continue for 1 mile to where Kingston Dyke passes under the road. Access to the river is on the right. Go over the gates and walk down either side of the dyke to the river.

Description: This stretch of the River Soar is quite under used but offers very good roach, bream and chub fishing for members that do fish it. From where Kingston Dyke flows into the main river the association have the rights to fish for 300 yards upstream (Beeby's Meadow) and 450 Yards downstream (Woodfield). Parking is only available at the roadside. The river is 300 Yards from the road.

Rules/Bans: No night fishing. Closed season 15th March to 15th June Inclusive.

Telephone: 0115 9199500

Facilities: None   **Sat Nav:** Not available

River Trent (Beeston)

Canal Side, Beeston, Nottingham.

Ticket Price: Day tickets £3.00. Concession £1.50. Nottingham AA run this stretch of river. Full Member £40.00. Disabled or over 65 £30.00. Juniors (age 15 or under) £10.00. Permits are available from local tackle shops. Closed season from the 15th March to the 31st April

Directions: From the A52 Dunkirk roundabout take the exit for Beeston Road/University Boulevard and continue for 1 mile. At the roundabout turn left into Queens Road and continue for ¾ mile to the traffic lights and turn left into Station Road. Continue along Station Road and into Meadow Lane for ¾ mile at the hump back bridge bear right into Canal Side. Continue along Canal Side for 500 yards. Parking is on surrounding roads. Access to the river is over the canal using the footbridge close to the locks.

Description: Just over 1.25 miles of fast, shallow water downstream of Beeston Weir. Chub and barbel are the dominant species directly below the weir with some roach and dace further downstream. The weir pool is also noted for pike.

Rules/Bans: No night fishing.

Telephone: 0115 9199500   **Sat Nav:** NG9 1NG

Facilities: None

River Trent (Bleasby)
Boat Lane, Bleasby.

NG14 7FT SAT NAV

Ticket Price: Day tickets £3.00. Concession £1.50. Nottingham AA run this stretch of river. Full Member £40.00. Disabled or over 65 £30.00. Juniors (age 15 or under) £10.00. Permits are available from local tackle shops. Closed season from the 15th March to the 31st April

Directions: From Lowdham roundabout take the A612 towards Southwell for 2 ½ miles. In Thurgarton Village turn right into Bleasby Road and continue for just under 1 mile to a sharp right bend into Station Road. Continue for just over 1 mile to the crossroads and go straight on into Boat Lane. Continue along Boat Lane for 600 Yards, parking is at the end of the lane. Access to the water is by walking 200 yards upstream.

Description: About 470 yards of river in a very picturesque setting. The stretch contains all the species of fish normally found in the Trent with roach and chub being predominant. For the large chub, leger a hair-rigged halibut pellet. Float anglers with waggler and stick float can do well, catching plenty of roach. Maggot is the best bait, use a mix of maggot and hemp for feeding.

Rules/Bans: No night fishing.   **Telephone:** 0115 9199500

Facilities: None   **Sat Nav:** NG14 7FT   43

River Trent (Holme)
Holme Lane, Winthorpe, Holme.

Ticket Price: Worksop District AA control this stretch of river. Adult tickets are £3.00. Under 16s and OAP's are £1.50 on the bank.

Directions: Leave the A1 at Newark and pick up the A46 heading to Lincoln. Follow the signs for Winthorpe village and turn right at the Lord Nelson pub. Go over the level crossing and look for the car parking sign for the Worksop District AA.

Description: There is a good head of bream which seem to stay in the centre of this steady flowing section of water. Try catching them using a groundbait feeder. Hair rig pellets work for the carp reaching 20lbs. Waggler fish for chub around 6lbs and plenty of roach to 1lb. I have seen anglers catching well using a long whip with caster & hemp.

Types of Fish: Carp to 20lbs, chub to 6lbs, perch to 2lb 9oz, bream to 8lbs, roach, barbel and pike.

Rules/Bans: Fishing dawn until dusk only. Traditional close season.

Facilities: Food outlet and toilet nearby.

Telephone: 01909 486350

Sat Nav: NG24 2NN to Lord Nelson pub nearby.

NOTTINGHAMSHIRE TACKLE SHOPS

Angling Supplies 49, Retford Rd, Worksop.	Tel: 01909 482974
Bridge Tackle 30, Derby Rd, Nottingham.	Tel: 0115 972 8338
East Midlands Angling 213, Station Rd, Mansfield.	Tel: 01623 744724
Fishing Synergy Ltd 469, Tamworth Rd, Nottingham.	Tel: 0115 972 2525
Future Fishing Willow Farm, Newark Rd, Newark.	Tel: 01636 612654
Gateford Angling Supplies 155, Gateford Rd, Worksop.	Tel: 01909 531115
Gerrys of Nottingham 96-100, Radford Boulevard, Nottingham	Tel: 0115 978 1695
Ians Angling Supplies 601, Chesterfield Rd North, Mansfield.	Tel: 07934 494500
Manor Baits Whyburn House, Whyburn Lane, Nottingham.	Tel: 0115 963 2188
Mansfield Angling Ltd 40, Layton Avenue, Mansfield	Tel: 01623 633790
Matchman Supplies 4, Ella Rd, Nottingham.	Tel: 0115 914 0210
Mill Tackle 85, Station Rd, Nottingham.	Tel: 01773 710679
Newark Angling Centre 29, Albert St, Newark.	Tel: 01636 686212
Openwater Angling Centre Ltd 50, Mansfield Rd, Mansfield.	Tel: 01623 627422
Peg 1 Angling Centre Church St East, Nottingham.	Tel: 01773 510324
Phil's Bait & Tackle Unit 2, Market Place, Sutton-In-Ashfield.	Tel: 01623 554654
Planet Carp 184, Alfreton Rd, Nottingham.	Tel: 0115 942 4941
Sparton Fishing Tackle Unit 2, Fields Farm Rd, Nottingham.	Tel: 0115 946 3572
Stapleford Angling 8, Archer Rd, Nottingham.	Tel: 0115 949 1812
Storm of Leicester 75, Victoria Rd, Nottingham.	Tel: 0115 9870525
Tacklebox Match Supplies Gressy Holme Farm, Bullpit Rd, Newark.	Tel: 01636 700117
The Matchmen 5, Bannerman Rd, Nottingham	Tel: 0115 927 8859
TJM Angling 3, Station St, Mansfield	Tel: 01623 628056
Used Tackle 6a, Annesley Rd, Nottingham.	Tel: 0115 963 4346
Victoria Tackle Centre 75, Victoria Road, Nottingham	Tel: 0115 987 0525
Walkers of Trowell 9-13, Nottingham Rd, Nottingham.	Tel: 0115 930 1816
Wriggly Buddies 10, The Camerons, Mansfield.	Tel: 07921 788861

Keep a record of all your fishing trips with

Log-it

Venue:		Address:				Date:
Peg No:	Start Time:		End Time:		Weather Conditions:	

Species	Weight	Method	Rig set up	Ground Bait	Hook Bait	Time

Venue:		Address:			Date:
Peg No:	Start Time:		End Time:	Weather Conditions:	

Species	Weight	Method	Rig set up	Ground Bait	Hook Bait	Time

Venue:		Address:			Date:
Peg No:	Start Time:		End Time:	Weather Conditions:	

Species	Weight	Method	Rig set up	Ground Bait	Hook Bait	Time

F I S H I N G   T E R M S

Here is a list of the words most commonly used. This will help anglers new to the sport to understand fishing terms used by other anglers.

BALE ARM: A revolving arm on a fixed spool reel which winds line onto the spool.

BAGGING UP: A term used when an angler is catching really well, or to describe a venue that is fishing well.

BAIT BANDS: These are small rubber bands. They are aimed at securing difficult to hook baits to the hook. They come in various sizes to accommodate the size of the bait.

BAITING NEEDLE: These pull the hair loop through the bait. They have a mechanism for attaching to the loop whether it is like a small hook, or a pivot that hooks over the loop. The needle is then drawn back through the bait taking the loop and hair with it.

BARBLESS: A type of hook without sharp barbs to help retain bait and fish. Barbed hooks are banned from most fisheries.

BIN LIDS: A slang term for large bream.

BITE ALARMS: These are electronic sensors that detect the movement of line caused by the fish. They usually have an audible alarm or light to alert the angler.

BIVIES: These are domed tents with an opening at the front providing a shelter from the elements.

BOILIES: These are generally hard balls of bait that are primarily designed as a carp bait.

BREAD PUNCH: A bread punch has a circular 'punch' at the end which is pushed down onto a slice of bread and cuts a small piece out which is placed on the hook. There are many different sizes of punches for different hook sizes.

BREAKING STRAIN: The amount of pressure a line will take before snapping.

BUMPED OFF: This term is used by pole anglers, whereby through the use of heavy tactics the fish once hooked is bumped off. This happens when the fish is not big enough to expand the elastic fully.

CASTERS: The chrysalis form of a maggot.

DEADBAITING: The use of dead fish for catching predatory fish such pike, perch, and eels.

DISGORGER: A long device to help remove the hook from a fish's mouth. Always have one with you.

FOUL HOOKED: A fish that has been hooked anywhere else on the body apart from the mouth.

GROUNDBAIT: A dry mixture intended to be thrown into the water to attract fish. Usually consists of bread crumb, crushed biscuit, crushed hemp or other ingredients.

HAIR RIG: A hair rig is generally a piece of line that extends beyond the point of the shank of the hook. On the end of the length of line is a small loop.

HOOKLENGTH: A short length of line, of lesser breaking strength than the mainline, to which the hook is tied. It is used to make it less likely to be detected by the fish. It also ensures that if the line is snapped by a fish, the angler would not then lose the float / swim feeder / leger and all the other shot

Legering: Bait held on the bottom by means of a weight or feeder.

Loosefeed: Small offerings of loose bait, such as maggots or sweetcorn, which are thrown into the water to keep the fish interested in the area you are fishing.

Line bites: False indications of bites usually caused by fish brushing against the line.

Lures: Artificial fish, used to tempt predators such as pike and zander.

Margin: This is an area nearest the bank, that has a shallower depth than that of the main water.

Match fishing: A competitive form of coarse fishing which involves people drawing out a random peg (a place to fish), and then trying to catch as many fish as possible within the allotted time. Usually the winner will be the one with the greatest weight of fish caught.

Peg: A peg is a pre defined fishing area. Venues are split up into evenly spaced fishing zones which are often marked with a wooden peg or marker.

Pinkies: The larvae of the green bottle fly. Small, very lively and great as a loosefeed on stillwaters and canals or as a hookbait for smaller fish.

Plummet: A device used for determining the depth of the water in which you are fishing.

Pole: A pole is constructed from very advanced carbon combinations and comes in various sizes, weight and prices.

Pole rig: These are lengths of line that have the float, weights and a hook attached.

Quiver tip: A special type of rod used to detect bites when ledgering. It has a sensitive tip that curves over when the angler has a bite. Quiver tips vary in strength and stiffness which can be changed according to the weather conditions.

Snags: Features in your swim that are likely to cause you problems They can also be fish holding features such as lilies, overhanging trees, sunken branches. A place to avoid once a fish is hooked.

Spade end hooks: Spade end hooks have an up-turned flattened piece of metal instead of an eye to which to tie the fishing line.

Specimen: A term given to any fish that is a particularly good size for its species.

Strike: To respond to the taking of the bait by pulling the rod in an upwards or sideways motion to hook the fish.

Swim: The area of water where you are fishing.

Tackle: A term used to refer to any fishing equipment (photo tackle)

Test curve: The test curve is the time and weight needed to make the tip bend 90 degrees from the rod butt. Each rod has a test curve with those being used for specimen fish such as carp having a greater test curve than a general coarse rod.

Trotting: Allowing a float to travel at the speed of the current.

Whip: This is a scaled down version of a pole.

I N D E X

page no.

A1 Pits (South Muskham Fisheries) 9
Aldercar Lane Fishery 10
Beeston Canal 11
Bestwood Duck Ponds 12
Covert Springs 13
Cranfleet Canal 14
Cromwell Lake Carp Fishery 15
Erewash Canal 16
Grantham Canal 17
Hackett Lakes 18
Hallcroft Fishery 19
Hawton Waters 20
Janson Fishery 21
Kings Mill Reservoir 22
Kodak Lakes 23
Lakeside Fishery 24
Langold Lake 25
L Lakes Fisheries 26
Little John Lakes 27
Lodge Farm Fisheries 28
Marnham Lake 29
Milestone Caravan Park 30
Moorgreen Carp & Coarse Fishery 31
Newark Dyke 49
Newlands Ponds 32
Oak Tree Lakes Fishery 33
Oldmoor Pond 34
Park Hall Lake 35
Pikes Oak Farm Fishing Lake 36
Portland Fishing Lakes 37
River Soar 51
River Trent (Beeston) 52
River Trent (Bleasby) 53
River Trent (Holme) 54
Sapphire Lakes 38
Sherwood Forest Fishery 39
Shireoaks Fishery 40
Smeaton's Lake 41
Spalford Fishery & Caravan Site 42
Sutton Lawn Dam 43
The Duffins 44
Wetlands Animal Park 45
Woodend Farm Complex 46
Woodetts Quarry Pond 47

If you know of a fishery that you would like including in one of these fish-it guides or you want to update an existing venue. Please fill in the form below.

Fishery Name

Fishery Address

Post code

Contact Name

Telephone No

| Adult Day Ticket Price | £ | concession OAP'S | £ |

Fish species and approximate weights

Brief Description

Rules / Bans

Facilities

Number of Lakes

Please e-mail or post a colour photo for inclusion in the next publication.

Please return this form to:
Arc Publishing
166 Knowle Lane,
Bents Green,
Sheffield S11 9SJ.

chris_keeling@tiscali.co.uk

New Fishery ☐

Update to Fishery ☐

New Fishery / Fishery Update Form

These regional fishing guides are packed with a wide range of information on lakes, ponds, canals, reservoirs and rivers. Each venue has a full colour page detailing all you need to know for a great days fishing. There are photos of each venue as well as useful tips on which peg to fish and best baits to use.